GILLIAN CLARKE

Ice

CARCANET

First published in Great Britain in 2012 by
Carcanet Press Limited
Alliance House
Cross Street
Manchester M2 7AQ

www.carcanet.co.uk

A CIP catalogue record for this book is available from the British Library

ISBN 978 1 84777 199 5

The publisher acknowledges financial assistance from the Arts Council of England

Supported by

**ARTS COUNCIL
ENGLAND**

Typeset by XL Publishing Services, Tiverton
Printed and bound in England by SRP Ltd, Exeter

To my cousin John Penri Evans, who took me back to Nant Mill

Acknowledgements

Acknowledgements are due to the following publications where some of these poems, versions or translations of them, first appeared: the *Guardian*; *Granta*; *Magma*; the *New Welsh Review*; *Roundy House*; *Taliesin*; *Touchstone*; *Love Poet, Carpenter: Michael Longley at Seventy*, edited by Robin Robertson (Enitharmon, 2009); *Jubilee Lines* (Faber, 2012) and *Ten Poems for Christmas* (Candlestick Press, 2012), both edited by Carol Ann Duffy.

I am grateful to the following for commissioning some of these poems, or where they were first heard: Abergavenny Food Festival; the Bevan Society; Cardiff University for the United Nations International Day of Older Persons; the Commonwealth Observance, Westminster Abbey 2010; LGBT History Week; Literature Wales; Llyfrgell Genedlaethol Cymru / the National Library of Wales; the Millennium Centre, Cardiff; Oriel Mostyn, Llandudno; Radio Devon; Radio Wales; the Royal Society of Architects in Wales and the RIBA Council meeting at the Senedd, March 2009; the Senedd / Welsh Assembly; the Smithsonian Festival of Washington DC; *Start the Week* (BBC Radio 4); the *Today* programme (BBC Radio 4); Pierre Wassenaar of Stride Treglown Architects and Gwent Archive; Welsh Water / Glâs Cymru.

Contents

Polar

Snowlight and sunlight, the lake glacial.
Too bright to open my eyes
in the dazzle and doze
of a distant January afternoon.

It's long ago and the house naps in the plush silence
of a house asleep, like absence,
I'm dreaming on the white bear's shoulder,
paddling the slow hours, my fingers in his fur.

His eyes are glass, each hair a needle of light.
He's pegged by his claws to the floor like a shirt on the line.
He is a soul. He is what death is. He is transparency,
a loosening floe on the sea.

But I want him alive.
I want him fierce
with belly and breath and growl and beating heart,
I want him dangerous,

I want to follow him over the snows
between the immaculate earth and now,
between the silence and the shot that rang
over the ice at the top of the globe,

when the map of the earth was something we knew by heart,
and they had not shot the bear,
had not loosed the ice,
had not, had not...

Ice

Where beech cast off her clothes
frost has got its knives out.

This is the chemistry of ice,
the stitchwork, the embroidery,
the froth and the flummery.

Light joins in. It has a point to make
about haloes and glories,
spectra and reflection.

It reflects on its own miracle,
the first imagined day
when the dark was blown

and there was light.

Advent Concert

Landâf Cathedral

First frost, November. World is steel,
a ghost of goose down feathering the air.
In the square, cars idle to their stalls, as cattle
remembering their place in the affair.
Headlamps bloom and die; a hullabaloo
dances on ice to the golden door.

Inside a choir of children sing, startled
at a rising hum over their shoulders
like a wind off the sea, boulders
rolled in the swell as, sweet and low,
Treorchy Male Voice Choir's basso profundo
whelms them in its flow and undertow,

and hearts hurt with the mystery,
the strange repeated story
of carol, candlelight and choir,
of something wild out there, white
bees of the Mabinogi at the window,
night swirling with a swarm of early snow.

Winter

When the white bear came from the north
its paws were roses,
its breath a garland,
its fur splinters of steel.

Where it lapped at the lip of the river,
water held its breath.
Where it trod, trees struck silver,
fields lay immaculate.

The river froze, and broke, and froze,
its heart slowed in its cage,
the moon a stone
in its throat.

The Geminids come and go.
Voyager crosses the far shores of space,
leaving us lonely,
stirred by story.

On the longest night the moon is full,
an answering antiphon
of dark and light.
In winter's cold eye, a star.

River

As if on its way to the sea
the river grew heavy,
a knife of pain in its heart,
slowed, slewed to a halt,

words slurred in its mouth
frozen in a dream of death,
came to, foot on the clutch,
engine running.

Struck dumb,
in a curb of ice
stilled in its sleep
under a hail of stars.

Where a river barge cuts upstream
in aching cold the surface cracks.
The drowned stir in their dream
as boat and boatman pass.

The shoals lie low,
silvers of elver, salmon like stones.
The backwash cuts the floe
to spars and bones,

the brimming ribcage
of a drowned beast.

Ice Music

Locked twelve floors up over the frozen Ely,
I show you the silver bones of the river
afloat on black water.

A hundred miles away, checking the sheep late,
you show me the light of the full moon through the larches
magnified in every lengthening snow-lens.

Stretched between us across the cryosphere,
white counties, fields, towns, motorway, blocked B roads,
the deepening geography of snow.

We both hear the music, the high far hum of ice,
strung sound, feather-fall, a sigh of rime,
fog-blurred syllables of trees, sap stilled to stone,

morning and evening, a moan of expanding ice
a timpani of plates colliding, a cry of icicles
tonguing the flutes of our tin roof.

Home for Christmas

A pause in the blizzard and you fetch me home
by motorway and marble corridor,
the last hill from Blaen Glowan slippery, slow,
the car crawls slipshod to the door.

Tonight we lie together listening
as miles of silence deepen to the coast.
Snow blinds the rooflights.
Roads forget themselves to north and east.

I sleep, wake, sleep again dreaming in stories,
turning, turning, landlocked in a myth,
our white room drifted deep
in moon-work of the silversmith.

All night a breath from the east
drives drifts off the fields through the avenue of beech
to fill the lane with waves of a frozen sea
so wild and still by morning nothing can pass.

We rise, dress, light fires, carry hay
to twelve ewes waiting hungry at the gate.
Birds gather in the garden for their feed
of crumbs, crusts, peelings, nuts and seed.

Our wild-tame neighbours, fellow inhabitants,
eye my scattering hands in hunger's silence.
I set soup simmering, dough rising in a bowl
as in the old days in our early glow,

like being new here, in this house, this place,
like being young and bold, bravely in love,
like staying alive and brazening out the ice
and snow, like being up for it, the shove

to sharpen up, to take the great adventure
of living the difficult day, the glamour.

Snow

We're brought to our senses, awake
to the black and whiteness of world.
Snow's sensational. It tastes
of ice and fire. Hold a handful of cold.

Ball it between your palms
to throw at the moon. Relish its plushy creak.
Shake blossoms from chestnut and beech,
gather its laundered linen in your arms.

A twig of witch hazel from the ghost–garden
burns like myrrh in this room. Listen!
Ice is whispering. Night darkens,
the mercury falls in the glass, glistening.

Motorways muffled in silence, lorries stranded
like dead birds, airports closed, trains trackless.
White paws lope the river on plates of ice
in the city's bewildered wilderness.

White Nights

In the luminous pages of the night,
under the deep drift of the duvet,
that silence like the world gone deaf.

In clouds of cold our bedroom holds its breath
like wartime winters. Roads unmake themselves
across a trackless land caught in the Mabinogi.

I'm wakeful, stalled by a stuttering line of verse.
By dawn, the garden hasn't stirred. Not a breath
shakes off the snow. Trees stand like death,

locked in that cold wedding in the story,
house, fields, in forever's frozen air.
Day after day the wait, weighted, bridal.

This is what Marged knew under this roof,
thatched then, I suppose, a hundred years ago,
quilt and *carthen* weighing her bones like stone,

hay-dust, cold, the sickness in her lungs, the knell
of the cow lowing to be milked, kicking its stall,
lamp and stove to light, on her last winter dawn.

carthen: a traditional Welsh blanket

trees stand in their bones
asleep in the creak of a wind
with snow on its mind.

Come spring they'll need reminding
how to weep, bleed, bud, grow rings
for cruck, or crib, or cross,

to break again in leaf.
The heartwood's stone, grief
of sap-tears frozen at the root.

While trees are dreaming green,
ice unfurls its foliage
on gutter, gate and hedge,

ghost-beauty cold as snow,
like the first forest, long ago.

Hunting the Wren

Darkness.
Dawn a wound in the east.
The garden's a ghost.

I set the kettle purring,
switch on the tree lights
in the glass-walled room.

Above the flight to Bethlehem,
the angels and cherubim,
the electric galaxies,

on the tree's top mast
something alive, a dark star,
a flutter of flight,

of bird-bewilderment.
A wren has dreamed a forest
multiplied in glass,

as tree dreamed bird into being,
its boughs and shadows spread
on a forest floor of snow.

I catch it in two hands,
a cup of wren,
release it to a frozen land.

Morning again and it's back,
a star of bird shit on the piano.
Good luck, my mother used to say.

Carol of the Birds

Winter sun is cold and low,
cry the kite and crake the crow,
bird of flame, bird of shadow,
ballad of blood on snow.

Owls are calling *llŵ, llŵ, llŵ,*
Kyrie, hullabaloo.

Small birds come without a sound,
starving to the feeding ground
where the robin with his wound
carols the ice-bound land.

Noctua, hibou, gwdihŵ,
owl's lullaby – who? who? who?

The story tells of pain and blood,
the troubles of a restless world,
a star that lights the snowy fields,
towards a newborn child.

Owls are calling *llŵ, llŵ, llŵ,*
Kyrie, hullabaloo,
noctua, hibou, gwdihŵ,
owl's lullaby – who? who? who?

Freeze 1947

Long ago in the first white world, school closed.
The park disappeared, the lake froze,
the town lost its way, sea struck dumb
on the beach. Birds held their tongues.

Land lay spellbound. World was an ice garden
beyond fern-frozen glass. Trees held out white arms,
waltzed with the wind and froze to stone.
On doorsteps bottled milk stood stunned.

The polar bear rug on the living room floor
rose from the dead, shook snow from its fur
and stood magnificent on all fours,
transfigured, breathing flowers.

And a girl on the road from school was stolen, her breath
a frozen rose, her marble sleep, death.
They hid the paper. 'Babe in the Wood' it said.
I thought of her school desk, its name-carved lid

slammed on slurred air, her face blurred
over books her eyes of ice would never read,
her china inkwell emptied of its words,
the groove for her pen like a shallow grave.

Freeze 2010

A girl found murdered by the road,
like detritus half-buried in the snow.

Grief howls in a suburban street, wild
as Demeter, who put the world to sleep,

a mother in perpetual winter weeps
for Persephone, her stolen child.

New Year

In the fields cold deepens in layers.
Sheeted in blizzard the farms drowse
in the dark, their living names ablaze
across the fields in golden windows.

Dead houses shut their blind eyes long ago.
Their dead lie ruined under snow.

See the footprint of the old school by the Glowan,
whose waters under the bridge chant children's games;
the wound of a forge, where still the field-name
rings with iron, the stamp of a hoof on stone.

List the farms, the fields all gone to earth,
the heroes, heroines; record the deaths
of beloved friend, lover, father, others
who fell to the gun, sickness, despair.

Incant their litany, make rosaries
of their names, tell their stories.
Inscribe their names in gold on rows
of slate like bedheads in the snow.

Marged Blaen Cwrt, poets of Sarnicol, Mounthill,
neighbours Tommy, Ithien, Angela,
and Simon, friend of poets, all now
fallen with the leaves, the falling snow,

or that mythic girl taken by Gwyn ap Nudd,
kept from her lover, locked away
like a corm in darkness, until winter eased
to spring and the lengthening day.

Captor and lover battled through the cold,
winter with spring, darkness with light.
till a blackbird sang in a blossoming blackthorn tree,
and winter let her go, and she was free.

The Dead after the Thaw

Starved birds in the snows of '47,
when no one had bread to spare.

A blackbird who sang all summer
stiff as a glove in the snow,

its eye not a gold ring,
but a pane of ice.

The swan who never came back from the dead
to her mate on the nest he rebuilt for her.

The old in city flats found three months dead,
in stinking garbage, a drift of junk mail, bills.

A poet dead with private cancer
in a country town.

The tramp they found in a field
after the thaw.

When they lifted him, meltwater
streamed from his open mouth.

Swans

She was brave in the bitter river,
the *Mary Rose*, doomed,
ice-chalice, lily in bloom.

Thaw, her feathers and bones dissolve in the flow
and she's gone, flower that floated
so light over death's undertow.

In lengthening light he patrols alone
ferocious on his watery shore
where the nest from last year and the year before

has drowned to a dredge of sticks and sludge.
In full sail, his body ablaze, bridge
over unfenced water, he waits for her.

The voice on the phone said,
'He doesn't know she's dead.
There is nothing to be done.'

Now love rides the river
like a king's ship, all wake and quiver,
and I can't tell him, it's over.

Who Killed the Swan?

'She is mine,' said the river
holding the swan on its palm like a lily.

Said the sky, 'She is mine to have and to hold,
my small white cloud of cold.'

'She is mine,' sighed the wind, wounding the air,
winnowing water, lifting a wing.

'Mine,' said the sun, noosing the swan
with a cold gold ring.

The cob swims in silence, its neck a question,
head downcast over water's mirror.

He lifts archangel wings to scorch the sky,
churning water and wind to rise

above the river, beating alone upstream.
'She is beside me, my soul, my dream,

the current under my heart.
Where I fly, she flies beneath me.'

The Newport Ship

Tatters of torn sails are gulls drifting
above the long brown muscles of the Usk
where the great ship slept five hundred years, a husk
embalmed in oils of alluvial mud and grit.

Hands that launch her now into the light of day
from the restless wrestling waters of Usk and Severn,
from the silt, the salt, the silence where she lay,
are tender as those who lift a broken man.

Now, just to see her, to imagine, is to hear
the clatter as men lapped planks to build the hull,
rang home the nails; and sailors drawn by the sea's pull
who crossed the unmapped wilderness of fear,

to beach on this shore. Ship without name abandoned
to the heave of tides, the scour of rain and wind,
she gives up her bones again like a queen unbound
from her winding-sheet, robed in sunlight, crowned.

Eiswein

Gathered in deepest winter before dawn,
fruit frozen to pearl, each milky stone
stared blind by last night's moon,

sweet water of the vine turned ice,
and ice turned liquid gold, a miracle
to quicken the dead and ferment the heart.

Alchemy of water, sugar, frost,
acids, aromas, and a weight of must,
remembered sweetness nourished in the dusks

of summer, like a lost language coming home,
the old words on the tongue, each one
a taste of earth, young rhubarb, honey, stone.

Ring each glass like a bell, and sip – as once
she'd sip her Christmas sherry from cut glass,
and sometimes, tripped by the tongue she had denied,

'*mêl*,' she'd say, '*melys*,' wine on her lip,
bemused by bee-songs from her father's fields,
the childhood taste of nectar sucked from clover,

as over the ford the river-syllables sang
turning the waterwheel at Nant Mill,
singing under the bridge, and singing still.

mêl: honey; *melys*: sweet

Thaw

Tonight the river's on the move
in a lovely backstroke, taking the tide
with a kick of silk thighs, shoulders

heaving the flood through flux
and fluency, stroking the keels
of coot and mallard, a single swan,

rocking a flock of gulls on its palm,
coupling grebe, boats at their mooring,
on currents swollen with melt
of mountain snows.

Fluent

Sleek as a girl in her silk, kissing goodnight
before slipping out to the dance, she'd leave her scent
on my pillow, the warmth of her skin on my cheek.
Cold pooled in the satin folds of her dress,
the glint of her rings, her animal wrap of fur,

and she's gone, night-river slipping its chains,
fluent, reflective, pulling to sea
under winter's weight, freighted
with ruin and wrack, a burden of birds, words
dead and alive, trees, driftwood, plastic,

and all my lost mountain syllables sing
on her frozen, loosening tongue
remembered, remembering.

Nant Mill

as if her broken words were scattered stones,
each course of the house unmade like a thought unspoken;
as if the walls, ruined in rampant sycamore,
were a language lost to a mumble of elder and bramble,
her story erased by too much silence;

as if she stood beside me checking the place
against the photograph – the field-gate at the bend
where the lane disappears, the cornerstone of the door
here where they stood, stilled on the threshold
in a new century before the wars;

as if the gap in the wall over the river
still held the butter churn, its paddle turning
where the current is slow with a secret dark,
then out with a shining song across the ford
where the horse's hooves once scattered water like sparks;

as if she left home one day, no turning back
and nothing to say; as if she might whisper again
the words for water, horse, mill, stream –
dŵr, ceffyl, melin, nant – in the tongue
the Clywedog has always sung.

Farmhouse

The house has gone to earth, slipped stone by stone,
lost to the power of trees to undo a wall,
unpick a roof slate by slate,

rain's alchemy to dissolve the bond in walls,
rot timbers beam by rafter, unmake dark rooms
where once ten children slept in feather beds,

three little ones together, Ceinwen, Elen, Vi,
cool curls, warm limbs across each other's bodies,
on icy air a scrawl of candle smoke,

the cold clouds of their breath. Gone,
rooms of daughters, a *croglofft* of five sons,
ovens of baking bread, cauldrons of *cawl*,

a ring of voices, hoof and clog on stone,
yr hen iaith's heartload of silence in the slant
of sun through trees, a wilderness lost for words.

croglofft: a room in the roofspace; *yr hen iaith*: the old language

Taid

Samuel Evans 1874–1940

It's carnival before the Great War,
the milk horse dressed in garlands, ribbons, rosettes,
the cart emblazoned: *Nant Mill Dairy*.
My grandfather stands a breathless moment
in hundred-year-old sunlight
for the slow click of the shutter.

The old house on his right, to his left
the Clywedog deep in trees below the road.
The reins run slack as water in his hands
as the secret flow of the river running
in black silence to break free
in shining small talk across the ford.

My three-year-old self remembers: Taid
in his chair by the fire in the big farm kitchen,
old man, black-browed, breath lost to emphysema
from a lifetime milling corn, taking my hand
to visit the stackyard with sugar for the horse –
was it Captain? or Belle?

I climb on the gate he leans on, one sugar lump
placed on my palm held under the velvet breath.
And one for me.
               Soon he was dead, died
in her arms, my mother said, her Data, my Taid,
as now the old house by the river has died
in the arms of sycamore and ash.

In Wern Graveyard

Thomas Evans 1826–1888, and Elizabeth 1832–1914

Their names scarcely legible, a verse in Welsh
erased by a century's dripping honeydews,
grave and graveyard lost to nettle and bramble,
all shape of it gone in a living scribble of trees.
I try to conjure and keep them, great-grandparents,
Thomas, Elizabeth, the miller and his wife,
long gone to earth, their bones absorbed in root
and thorn, wild flowers, the secret life
of birds. Our flesh and blood. Our DNA.
Mine. John's. Will's. We bear them in mind,
scrambling through thorn and thicket to the car
and home to the farm where every day will end
and begin with the moan of the cattle's song
as they sway to their stalls for milking.

Lambs

Thaw. The breaking of waters,
a breath of frost on the night grass,
the give of earth underfoot.
We're up early and late,
for these are the blood-days.

In the field corner a ewe is restless,
turning, treading her nest of pain,
absorbed with nothing but the birth
her body's ocean brings.
Her waters smell like the sea.

She drinks him, his bubbling cries,
her voice a soft low growl,
strains again and a second lamb
comes slippery as a fish in a stream,
steaming in moonlight.

We leave them an hour then tempt her in,
one lamb each dangled before her,
their hearts in our hands.
She follows dancing, butting us
all the way to the pen,

nudges them to suckle, stamps us away,
settles to small talk, fresh water, hay.

The Letter

from Gwyneth Benbow

I live her memory as if it were my own:
a path through woods and four girls racing down
– Gwyneth, Elen, Ceinwen, Vi – three sisters and a friend
whose letter out of the blue brought scent and sound
of a long ago spring day between the wars:

a river rippling stones, laughter of girls,
skelter of skirts into the kitchen at Nant Mill.
Two older sisters set the great elm table,
loaves cool on a rack, churned butter gleams,
five handsome brothers tramp in from the fields.

All over the world a child's still running home
through grim street, grimy ginnel, field or slum.
Inside the old ones, ending their century,
the child who was, alive in memory,
and who they were, lover, mother, hero.

Some lose themselves and us before they go.
Some live as if they had all the time in the world
to brave out frailty and pain, still panning for gold.

Grebes

They tread water, breast to breast on the Ely,
feeding each other delicacies from the deep.
Purge me with hyssop. *Asperges me.*
Bring me water asparagus,
tongues of manna, passion fruit, love-juice,
buds and blood-beads of pomegranate.

Out on the river's a wedding of water and light.
Bicycle bells in the close
calling to avenue, *heol* and hill,
a humdrum of cars on the overpass,
the blackbird's solo in a willow
to the back garden psalm of the city.

They couple tiptoe on the river's sleeve,
saliva and silvers of weed,
heart to heart, bill to bill.
In her delicate crate of bone the future
is waking, seed's clutch of stars
to quicken in the curve of the dark

for the nest they'll weave on the water,
a raft of stems tethered to a reed.

heol: road

Burnet Moths

We walk the old dog on Grangemoor hill
raised on a city's waste, the filth of landfill.
Her tail's a flag of joy waving though grasses,
a blur of butterflies, larksong, and all the pleasure
a generous day can give to human and dog
walking a meadow nourished on trash and decay.

By the path, bound to grass stems, spindles of spit,
chrysalids, papery, golden, torn, unfurling
sails of damp creased silk, spinnakers filling
with breath, burnet moth wings of scarlet and black
like opera stars who live and love and die
in an hour on the flight of an aria.

Now it's her turn to die, her beautiful head on my knee,
her life an infinity still, till the sedative takes,
and she crumples to sleep at my feet, folded back
to before she was born. The kind vet waits.
Sleep isn't death. Then the needle, barbiturate
straight to the heart. Here – and gone.

Er Gwell, Er Gwaeth

a'r fodrwy hon y'th briodaf...
Something about the ring in the blackbird's eye
on an April evening; the raptor's jewelled stare;
the marriage of sun and rain on dancing water;
the circle of my arms round sheets off the line;
yours bringing armfuls of wood for the fire.

â'm corff y'th anrhydeddaf...
Something of touch, taste, tongue, the language
of hands, those chemical gifts one to the other;
grace and gesture, silence, reflection,
that pair for life two swans on a river
soundlessly sculling the stream, lover to lover.

â'm holl olud bydol y'th gynnysgaeddaf...
My dowry a derelict house on a hill, five fields,
two acres of bluebells under oaks; yours, a vision.
You made sound the ruin, dreamed space and light,
a room of oak and glass, let in the sky, the hills,
and all of Ceredigion, *Cariad*, in a glance.

Er Gwell, Er Gwaeth: For Better, For Worse; *a'r fodrwy hon y'th briodaf*:
with this ring I thee wed; *â'm corff y'th anrhydeddaf*: with my body I thee
worship; *â'm holl olud bydol y'th gynnysgaeddaf*: with all my worldly goods I
thee endow; *Cariad*: darling

Honesty

for Imtiaz Dharker

A flourish of flowers self-seeded
in the shade of an old wall,
nourished on nothing but stone,
dirt, detritus, winter's tears.

From a mulch of dead things
comes a rush of stems,
heart-shaped leaves, Earth's love-gift,
the opulent purples of April,

to keep in the dark when it's over
a purse of seed translucent as bees' wings,
as pages of old books,
as the silver eyes of your lover.

You show me the way it is, to lose, to keep
the light of your life in the lens of a line,
syllables of grief, the world
more luminous seen through tears.

Bluebells

Which came first? Scent or heartburst of blues?
Cerulean, indigo, sky, a breath of rain,
sunlight between stems of sessile oaks

before the wood breaks leaf, when trees first feel
a quickening in their roots – the shift and stir
of bulbs swelling beneath the earth.

The ink-blue dark of an icy night of stars,
last snow gone from the shadowed side of a wood:
Porthkerry, Fforest, Allt Blaen Cwrt.

Or long ago when folds of a satin dance-dress
fell about me like a drench of water
when I hid in her dark wardrobe from their storms.

Or the sweet still blues of La Parisienne's gown,
in one of those still hours in the gallery,
and I a child alone in a room of treasure.

After the bitter cold it comes again,
this dream of blue breaking in the wood
in a long flood about the ankles of oaks,

the drowning satins of cool blue in a wardrobe,
beauty and grief and every blue in the world
in each drooping head of bells.

La Parisienne: the painting by Renoir in the Welsh National Museum and
National Museum of Art, Cardiff

Between the Pages

for John Pikoulis

A long-ago Saturday,
tyres spinning the light
and the wind in our hair.
Two cycling to nowhere,
lost in the lanes between
Penarth and somewhere.

We stopped by a stone church,
dropped in cool grass, wheels
milling gold as they slowed,
drank from our cupped hands
from the tap by the door
for the tenders of graves.

And this is for you, John,
man of letters, of lives:
inside, in the watery shadows,
I climbed the pulpit with a fistful
of primroses, opened the Bible,
its pages cold as a wave,

pressed my flowers in its depths.
I was twelve, the page 248.

Glâs

A little rill of rainwater off the fields
is plucking its harp strings in the sun,
and a ditch among reeds is a rising gleam,
the miracle of water's give and yield.

Two mingling colours of *glâs* in a stream,
and I'm dreaming that secret web of water
underfoot, down through the storeyed strata
in Earth's unmappable corridors of stone.

While along the road the whistling water-gods,
sons of Coventina, goddess of springs and wells,
are burying miles of piping like a map
of life, an arterial stream to every tap,

like those rivers, reservoirs, aquifers underground,
invisible silvers silent as ultrasound.

glâs: blue or green

Small Blue Butterfly

Six years old, with my father, waving to sailors
in the heat of a long ago summer, leaping the rails
as a big ship docked, steadied and slowly rose
on the rolling tide when the sea-gates closed.

Dizzy with tar, salt, coal, the river
lost in the throat of the Severn, and just here, a quiver
above the muscular mud, the colour of sky
over the Bay, a small blue butterfly.

I think of its frail flight over shifting silts
as I climb the steps, slate firm underfoot,
like climbing the centuries, leaving the lift and lilt
of opposing currents a long way out.

After eight hundred years adrift,
and all the years of my life on the way to this,
I claim this house as my own,
climbing the steps, coming home.

this house: Y Senedd, the Welsh Assembly building

Mango

Paring the mango tonight, my knife so sharp
I took off the skin in a single ringlet, green
with a flush of rose — and I half remembered
boarding a white ship, grown-up talk of war.

Only this stays — me in my father's arms,
carried aboard a big ship in the docks,
my mother behind us pretty in blue,
my father's friend, the Captain, at the rail.

Down in the cabin they laid me to sleep
on a bed that rocked. The sea looked in
through the window. Then it was dark.
There were secrets. The Captain's eyes were kind.

He gave me a fruit like a cold green stone so big
it overflowed my two hands cupped together.
They cut the top, and I sucked it, drank it, juice
running down my chin, my fingers, my dress.

It wasn't like plums, blackberries, our worm-hearted apples.
It was like a fruit in a book sucked by a boy
in a faraway land you could only reach on a ship
sailed over a huge blue ocean. Only this remains —

the taste and the rocking sea, the fruit like a stone
with a stone inside like the keel of a little ship,
storm-rocked with grown-up whispers, my globe spinning,
the load in the hold and our hearts heavy, shifting.

Senedd

Mountains spent time on it:
the slow settlement of silts,
mudstones metamorphosed to slate,
prehistory pressed in its pages.

Rock blown from the quarry face
and slabbed for a plinth, a floor,
a flight of stairs rising
straight from the sea.

The forest dreamed it:
parable or parabola.
Look up into the gills of fungi,
the throat of a lily.

A man imagined it:
the oak roof's geometry
fluid and ribbed as the tides
in their flux and flow.

He cools us with roof-pools of rain
that flicker with light twice reflected,
a wind-tower of steel to swallow our words
and exchange them for airs off the Bay.

Inside the house of light at the sea's rim
you can still hear the forest breathe,
feel the mountain shift underfoot,
hear sands sift in the glass.

The Tree

after Red Cuts *by David Nash*

for Oriel Mostyn Gallery, Llandudno

The architect's vision, a space in the mind
before a line was drawn or walls imagined,

is a poem before sound, before words,
before the sea-lit ceilings shadowed by birds,

bare concrete printed with the memory
of trees grown with a forest's slow geometry.

Workmen tapped things home with a final touch,
tuning the building to its perfect pitch.

Builders with art on their arms are done,
whistling brickies, carpenters, masons gone.

The tree, old yew, placed at the heart of the gallery,
glorious, broken, bloody, ablaze, a glare

of flame alive in its dance of death,
art's sign, and metaphor, and shibboleth.

Blue Sky Thinking

April 2010

Let's do this again, ground the planes for a while
and leave the runways to the racing hare,
the evening sky to Venus and a moon
so new it's hardly there.

Miss the deal, the meeting, the wedding in Brazil.
Leave the shadowless Atlantic to the whale,
its song the only sound sounding the deep
except the ocean swaying on its stem.

Let swarms of jets at quiet airports sleep.
The sky's not been this clean since I was born.
Nothing's overhead but pure blue silence
and skylarks spiralling into infinite space,

a pair of red kites flaunting in the air.
No mark, no plane-trail, jet-growl anywhere.

A Wind from Africa

Was it reading the butterfly book in the garden,
the poetry of Lepidoptera,
the common verse of the field?
Gatekeeper. Meadow Brown. Small Heath.
Orange Tip. Ringlet. Marsh Fritillary.

Was it a flick of the Gulf Stream's tail, the must
of lion breath, that southern wind that brings
swallows and clouds of red Saharan dust
that made the beech tree suddenly sing
with a thousand flickering wings?

The tree dizzy with dancers, manifold
desert reds, Moroccan gold,
Painted Ladies – on an Odyssey
from Africa, wings on the wind
over continents and seas.

All summer they lingered, feeding, for all we knew
on our burdock and thistles, sipping rain and honeydew.
They live to breed, be beautiful and die.
All winter, ghost butterflies in the tree,
and snow, white wings falling from the sky.

Running Away to the Sea — 1955

It might have been heatstroke, the unfocused flame of desire
for a name in a book, a face on the screen, the anonymous
object of love. Two schoolgirls running like wildfire,
bunking off through dunes to the sea, breathless.

We were lost and free, East of Eden.
It was James Dean, Elvis, Bill Haley and the Comets.
It was Heartbreak Hotel on the gramophone.
It was Heathcliff by torchlight in bed after lights-out.

The dunes were molten glass. We slowed to a dawdle,
rippling sand with our toes, grains of gold
through our fingers, on our skin, in our hair,
without words to say why, or who, or where.

This I remember. The hour was still, bees
browsing sea lavender, and beyond the dunes
the channel as blue as the Gulf of Araby,
a name from the drowse of a daydreaming lesson,

sun on the board, the chalk, Sister's hand, a far-away
voice, as if heard through water, murmuring rosaries:
Egypt, the Red Sea, the Bitter Lakes, Suez.
A psalm of biblical names called Geography.

That was the last day the world stood still. In a year
there'd be tanks in Budapest, over Sinai bombers on the move,
and I'd be in the streets on the march against war,
as empires loosened their grip. It was almost like love.

Pheidippedes' Daughter

for Catrin

Long silver girl who slipped easy
and early from the womb's waters,
whose child-breath was a bird in a cage,
the inhaler in her fist her amulet,

grew tall, beautiful, caught her breath,
outran the hound, the hare, the myth,
the otter, salmon, swallow, hawk,
the river, the road, the track.

She texts again — this time Santiago.
She's counting seven cities underfoot,
running the bloodlines of language, lineage,
for Ceridwen's drop of gold, an ear of corn,

to leave the Battle of Marathon and run
through pain and joy with news to the gates of a city,
to arrive at the finishing line, and say,
'*Nenikékamen* — We have won.'

Storm-Snake

A day of summer heat
in central France, breathless before storm,
then a stir of wind like the whispering of wheat
or rosaries, the black sky warm

above a million hectares of fertility.
A sudden growl of warning in the stones,
over the mountains, serpents of electricity,
unease as old as Eden.

The storm breaks shimmering over Limousin,
the sound of weighty matter heaved across
the floor of heaven, till earth is diamond,
and here on the road, belly up, crushed,

a little silver snake, like lightning's memory,
someone's initial signed on an old story.

Oradour, 10 June 1944

Silence in the empty streets, the square,
the shuttered houses, sun-blind boulangerie,
dressmaker, surgery, school, Mairie.

At the oil-clothed table in the shade of a vine,
Madame Roufanche is pouring a rough red wine,
ladling cassoulet into yellow bowls,
with a crusty cheese, an armful of warm loaves
brought home that morning, the dew still
on the fields, her quilt like a cloud on the sill.

We could have been here, passing through, like now,
could have risen, restored, in love, from the bed
in the room overlooking the square, could have shared
her table, her man home from work, a nod, nothing said,
could have talked in French, in smiles, in gesturing hands,
in the raise and ring of glasses, the breaking of bread.

That long ago summer the house, the church, the dead
in their graves, the streets, the square, all spread
under the linen of silence, sunlight, noon,
waiting for boots, orders, the struck match, the gun,
the church full of women fired, men in the burning barn,
and safe in the future, we and our love not born.

A Glory in Llanberis Pass

In the dream I walk the path again,
up, up in the mist and rain,
heart and foot springing in sparse light,
eyes down, foot, scree, foot, turf, foot, stone,

to rise through the glory like a salmon leaping the falls,
up, up through a hole in the sky, a ring of fire,
a rainbow like an oriel window,
the iris of God's eye.

Shearwaters on Enlli

for Michael Longley

Michael, the oldest known ringed bird
is a Manx shearwater, near sixty and going strong.
I choose it as *llatai*, bird-messenger, sea-crier
for the poet of flight and song.

Midnight, midsummer, and almost dark
but for the loom of Dublin at the rim of the world,
flocks of shearwaters home in from the sea,
like the souls of twenty thousand saints
come to reclaim their holy remains.

They flare in the sweep of the lighthouse beam,
a sigh of sparks, an outcry of angels, a scream
as if they feel it, the shock of the light
then the dark after the long day's flight
in the troughs of the waves.

Doused one by one, each footless bird to its burrow.
And I to mine, a damp nest in the lighthouse,
every swing of the beam a wing feathered with gold
fires the room all night, a blaze against the cold.

Enlli: Bardsey Island

White Cattle of Dinefwr

Ghosting the valley still, ten centuries
since the time of Hywel Dda, their dreaming heads
sway below the castle and Black Mountain
against the sky.

Luminous as white flowers
at dusk, a thousand years of moonlight,
their legendary silver lit dark times
before power fired the windows of the house.

Like sewin silvering upstream to spawn
in Tywi and its tributary streams,
white fire, electric, veins of history,
the cattle innocent of their lineage,

how it moves us, brings to mind our story –
Rhodri Mawr, the Lord Rhys, Hywel Dda –
grazing dusk pastures,
pale as the first stars.

Six Bells

for the forty-four miners killed in the explosion on 28 June 1960

Perhaps a woman hanging out the wash
paused, hearing something, a sudden hush,

a pulse inside the earth like a blow to the heart,
holding in her arms the wet weight

of her wedding sheets, his shirts. Perhaps
heads lifted from the work of scrubbing steps,

hands stilled from wringing rainbows onto slate,
while below the town, deep in the pit

a rock-fall struck a spark from steel, and fired
the void, punched through the mine a fist

of blazing firedamp. As they died,
perhaps a silence, before sirens cried,

before the people gathered in the street,
before she'd finished hanging out her sheets.

Sarah at Plâs Newydd, Llangollen, 5 July 1788

I leave dear Eleanor at her desk, writing
her letters to the world in the dawn light,
and walk the morning relishing the hour –
birdsong, roses wet from a night of rain.
Maiden's Blush. Rosa Mundi. Rose d'Amour.

Loosed from the shippon the cows sway down the lane.
The maids sing at their work. Mary brings buttermilk,
a pat of butter glistening from the churn,
for the Bishop of St Asaph comes at nine
to breakfast with us, talk, and walk the garden.

And so we live, and cultivate land and mind.
We read, write, study, make beautiful
a house and garden. Poets and men of letters
visit us – Wordsworth, Byron, Shelley,
the Duke of Wellington, Sir Walter Scott.

Our neighbours too, who took us in from the storm,
the hounds of disapproval at our heels,
when we reached this sheltering valley and this house.
Come. See our vines, our roses. Be our witness
how honest love can shape the wilderness.

Sarah and Eleanor: Sarah Ponsonby and Eleanor Butler, the Ladies of
Llangollen

Pebble

Weigh two hundred million years
in your hand, the mystery of eras,
a single syllable
pulsing in a pebble.

It quivers in your palm
like the heartbeat of a hare in its form,
with the shindig of ocean, ancient landslips,
rock-fall, storm, the sea's and centuries' lapse.

Take in your right hand from the evening sky
that other sad old stone, the moon.
You, Earth, pebble, moon-stone,
held together in the noose of gravity.

Feel the beach shift underfoot, the planet turn,
all Earth's story in a stone.

Taliesin

Frank Lloyd Wright 1867–1959

A house on a hill, Spring Green, Wisconsin.
From an outcrop of rock, an outcry of water,
he would curb the stone, harness the light of the sun,
bridle the great horse of the river,
raise walls, wings, walkways, terraces, a tower,
slabbed stone horizons on the shining brow.

The mark was on him before birth,
that single drop of gold his mother brought
across the Atlantic in the hold of her heart
from the old home in Ceredigion,
for her imagined boy, her child,
man of her making who would shape a world.

Raised in the old language, the old stories,
he learned his lines from the growth-rings of trees,
wind over water, sandbars, river-currents,
rhythms of rock beneath the ground he stood on,
colours of the earth, his favourite red
the rusting zinc of old Welsh barns, of *twlc* and *beudy*.

Taliesin, house of light, of space and vista,
corners for contemplation, halls for fiesta.
He sang a new architecture
from the old, in perfect metre.

twlc and *beudy*: pigsty and cow house

60

August Hare

It's all ears for the strung deeps
of aquifers and springs,

the almost silent arpeggios of the stream,
harp-strings of grasses brushed in passing,

a gasp of pen on paper, rasp
of grasshopper song in the field,

August's breath in the beech tree,
acer wringing her hands,

and the dry sound of chestnut
fingering the wind.

Gleision

for the four miners killed at Gleision drift mine, 15 September 2011

Colours of mountain light, greens, greys,
blues of distance, dusk's lavenders.
Glâs of rivers and rain and waterways
where streams and heroes are lost
in the hill's dark hollowed heart,

and nothing's left but black of the bleak 'if only',
the never again of men trapped in the pit
while women wait, and world grows lonely
at the slow procession of the hours, dread
of the imagined and remembered dead.

gleision: the plural of *glâs*, blue or green

Osprey

Suddenly from the sea
a migrating angel on its way
from Lapland to Africa
took a break at Cwmtydu.
It stayed three weeks
like the moon roosting in an oak.

They fed it like a pet
on buckets of slippery silver
left over from the fish shop.
You could tell it was happy
by the way it splintered the sun
with its snowbird wings.

But its mind was on Africa,
the glittering oceans, the latitudes
sliding beneath its heart.
'Stay!' they said. 'Stay!'
But one day it lifted off and turned south
for the red desert, for the red sun.

Wild Plums

The old trees lean together
one in the arms of the other,
mossed, wind-broken, snag-branched,
seeded a century back by chance.

Our first spring – remember? –
starbursts of petals
from stubborn wood that April,
and every September

sweet nameless plums
to pick from the air as we pass.
At night fruit thudding in grass
is the drumbeat of dreams.

Blue-skinned, gold-fleshed,
simmered and stored in sugar and spice
till a time of thaw, prunus fresh
on the tongue, a tingle of ice.

Harvest Moon

You called me out to the lane – come quick! –
when the red moon rose in a smoking cloud over Pisgah
like a house on a far mountain helplessly burning,

and the stubble fields on the valley slope ablaze,
august and auburn in the last light of the sun
and the first light of the moon.

If I close my eyes now it's still there, glorious,
and you in the lane watching the golden fields.
When I open them, going, going, gone...

Blue Hydrangeas

You bring them in, a trug of thundercloud,
neglected in long grass and the sulk
of a wet summer. Now a weight of wet silk
in my arms like her blue dress, a load

of night-inks shaken from their hair —
her hair a flame, a shadow against light
as long ago she leaned to kiss goodnight
when downstairs was a bright elsewhere

like a lost bush of blue hydrangeas.
You found them, lovely, silky, dangerous,
their lapis lazulis, their indigos
tidemarked and freckled with the rose

of death, beautiful in decline.
I touch my mother's skin. Touch mine.

In the Reading Room

He scans the stream, silver-eyed as a heron
searching the surface for what might betray
a halt in the flow, pentameter's delay,
a master's faded words, his lexicon.

Before him, found in an old book
marking a page, a longhand manuscript.
Look, where the nib unloaded ink and dipped
and rose again, leaving a blot on the downstroke,

writing by candlelight in another century,
wind in the chimney, maybe, the pen's small sound.
He writes: 'Anonymous. Date a mystery.
Some words illegible. No signature found.'

Yet the poem sings in his mind from the silent archive
and all the dead words speak, aloud, alive.

The Plumber

Harry Patch 1898–2009

He'd often work crouched on the floor
his toolbag agape beside him
like a wound.

He'd choose spanner or wrench,
tap for an airlock, blockage, leak,
for water's sound.

Not a man for talk. His work
a translation, his a clean trade
for silent hands.

Sweet water washed away waste,
the mud, the blood, the dirt,
the dead, the drowned,

the outcry, outfall, outrage of war
transformed
to holy ground.

Listen

to the chant that tranced me thirty years ago
in Samarkand: the call to prayer at dawn;

to that voice again, years and miles from then,
in the blood-red mountains of Afghanistan;

to the secret placing of a double-bomb
at a dark hour in a dusty street;

to the first foot to tread the viper's head,
the scream that ripped the morning's rising heat;

to the widow's wail as she crouches in the rubble
over a son, a brother torn apart;

to a mother dumb with shock who locks her door
and sits alone, taking the news to heart;

to the soldier's words, it's World War One out here;
to the rattled air, the growl of the grenade;

to a chanting crowd fisting the foetid air;
to a silent town at a funeral parade;

to ruin ripening in poppy fields;
to barley burnished in the summer air;

to the sound at dusk, cantata of despair,
the holy call become a howl of prayer.

The March

for my late father-in-law, Glyndwr Thomas, miner, Oakdale colliery

Boots and rain drummed the tram roads,
that bitter night in 1839,
potholed and stumbled with mud and stones.
Five thousand men, workers in iron and coal
from mine and furnace, Sirhowy, Ebbw, Rhymni,
heads bowed against the storm like mountain ponies.

Their bones ached from the shift, wind in the shaft,
the heat of the furnaces. Yet on they marched,
their minds ablaze because their cause was right,
through darkness from Ebbw Vale, Blackwood, Pontypool,
faces frozen and stung by the lash of rain,
trudging the roads to Newport through the night.

At the Welsh Oak, Rogerstone, betrayed by daylight,
Frost's men from the west, Williams's from the east,
Jones's men never arrived. The rest struck on
to stand, single-hearted in the square
before the Westgate. Had they stood silent then,
had they not surged forward, had not been shaken

by rage against injustice, had they muzzled
the soldiers' muskets with a multitude
of silence, had reason spoken,
those steely thousands might have won the day.
But they stormed the doors to set their comrades free,
and shots were fired, and freedom's dream was broken.

A score dead. Fifty wounded. Their leaders tried,
condemned, transported. The movement, in disarray,
lost fifty years. Then came at last that shift
of power, one spoonful of thin gruel at a time,
from strong to weak, from rich to poor,
from men to women, like a grudged gift.

Archive

They left their mark on pages, stones,
between Usk and Wye, Ebbw, Monnow, bones
in the turned earth of a field, in pit and street,
list and litany, letter, will, receipt,
the etcetera of terraces, a statued square,
all that was left behind of who they were.

Ysgrifen yr afonydd, sibrwd Sirhywi,
Rhymni, Wysg, Gwy ac Ebwy,
geiriau o gariad, stôr o straeon,
gwaith glô, gwaith haearn,
gwaith tir mewn gwynt a glaw,
deilen a dalen yn yr adeilad hwn.

Read in these walls, these pages, history
between the lines of what's most ordinary.

Ysgrifen yr afonydd...:

Scribble of rivers, whisper of Sirhywi,
Rhymney, Usk, Wye and Ebbw,
words of love, a store of stories,
coal-work, iron-work,
land-work in wind and rain,
on leaf and page in this house.

The Book of Aneirin

Sorrow sharp as yesterday, a lament
passed down and learned by heart
until that moment
when the scribe began to write.

Fifteen centuries later,
words still hymn their worth,
young men, all but one slaughtered,
lost in the hills of the Old North.

Blood-ballad
of the battlefield,
on quires of quiet pages, laid leaf
on leaf like strata of stone, Aneirin's grief.

The Book of Aneirin: the thirteenth-century manuscript of a sixth-century
poem

Lament for Haiti

For the ground that shivered its skin like an old horse,
for the shout of the sun,
the cry of the earth as it broke its heart,
the palace that fell into itself like snow.

For the hospital with its rows of white graves.
For the cathedral that folded on emptiness calling God's name as
it went.
For its psalms of sorrow,
the prayers of the living and dead.

For each crushed house, its cots, cushions and cups,
cooking pots pressed between pages of stone.
For the small lung of air that kept someone alive,
for the rescuer's hand, for the slip of a life from its grip.

For the smile of daylight
on a woman's face,
for her daughter dead in the dark.
For the baby born in the rubble.

For tomorrow's whistling workmen
with their hods of bricks
For scaffolding and walls rising out of the grave
over rosaries of bones.

The Fish Pass

This looks like dreaming – the silk lagoon
reflective with sails, hotels, a flight of gulls,
havened from Severn heaving at the wall.
The rising tide's the longhand of the moon.

We lean where broken rivers slice the sluice,
Taff and Ely, swollen by upland springs,
now slatternly with silt, out on the loose,
a joyous weight of waters gathering.

The homing salmon hurls against the force,
sensing the sweet in the salt – *dŵr, afon* –
a line and lure from the mountain water course
in its cold blood like love. Silver and driven

it leaps through air, weir, waterfall to spawn
in shallows of the stream where it was born.

afon: river

74

Ode to Winter

We hoard light, hunkered in holt and burrow,
in cave, *cwtsh*, den, earth, hut, lair.
Sun blinks. Trees take down their hair.
Dusk wipes horizons, seeps into the room,
the last flame of geranium in the gloom.

In the shortening day, bring in the late flowers
to crisp in a vase, beech to break into leaf,
a branch of larch. Take winter by the throat.
Feed the common birds, tits and finches,
the spotted woodpecker in his opera coat.

Let's learn to love the icy winter moon,
or moonless dark and winter constellations,
Jupiter's glow, a slow, incoming plane,
neighbourly windows, someone's flickering screen,
a lamp-lit page, drawn curtains.

Let us praise intimacy, talk and books,
music and silence, wind and rain,
the beautiful bones of trees, taste of cold air,
darkening fields, the glittering city,
that winter longing, *hiraeth*, something like prayer.

Under the stilled heartbeat of trees,
wind-snapped branches, mulch and root,
a million bluebell bulbs lie low
ready to flare in lengthening light,
after the dark, the frozen earth, the snow.

Out there, fox and buzzard, kite and crow
are clearing the ground for the myth.
On the darkest day bring in the tree,
cool and pungent as forest. Turn up the music.
Pour us a glass. Dress the house in pagan finery.

The flown, the fallen,
the golden ones,
the deciduous dead, all gone
to ground, to dust, to sand,
borne on the shoulders of the wind.

Listen! They are whispering
now while the world talks,
and the ice melts,
and the seas rise.
Look at the trees!

Every leaf-scar is a bud
expecting a future.
The earth speaks in parables.
The burning bush. The rainbow.
Promises. Promises.